The Story of
BABY MOSES

Retold by Susan Dickinson
Illustrated by Sally Holmes

CARNIVAL

One night a Hebrew woman who was living in Egypt gave birth to a lovely baby boy. He was the most beautiful baby she had ever seen, but as she held him in her arms, tears ran down her cheeks.

The Egyptians had ordered that all
baby boys born to Hebrew mothers
were to be thrown into the River
Nile.

"I cannot throw my baby into the river!" she cried. "Why are the Egyptians so cruel to us?" "Because they are afraid of us," said her husband. "They think there are too many of us."

With the help of her daughter, Miriam, the mother managed to hide her little son for three months.

But when he was three months old
he was getting too big to be hidden
away, so his mother went to the edge
of the river and gathered armfuls of
reeds and rushes.

She wove the rushes into a hooded
cradle, which she covered all over
with tar to make it watertight. Then
she kissed her baby and laid him
gently inside.

She and Miriam carefully placed the cradle among the rushes at the side of the river. Then she said to Miriam: "Wait here and watch over the baby. But don't let anybody see you. I must go home, in case somebody guesses that he belongs to me."

Miriam crouched down among the reeds at the water's edge. After a little while she heard the sound of voices. She peeped out and saw the Egyptian princess coming down to the river to bathe with her maids.

The princess was just about to step into the water when she suddenly spied the strange black object floating a little way away.

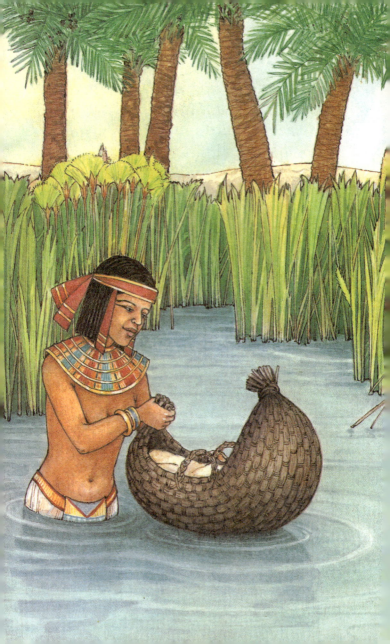

She sent her maidservant to look,
and the girl brought the cradle to the
princess.

The princess lifted the cover and there was the little baby, sleeping peacefully. "What a lovely baby!" she said. "Surely he must belong to one of the Hebrew women. How dreadful for his poor mother to have to leave him here in this floating cradle. But whatever shall we do? We cannot take him home as Father would order him to be thrown into the Nile."

At that moment, Miriam ran up.
"Excuse me, your Highness," she
said. "Would you like me to find
someone to look after the baby?"
"Oh, yes, please," said the princess.
"I was wondering whatever we could
do."

Miriam ran home and told her
mother what had happened.
Together, they ran back to the river
where the princess was playing with
their baby.

The princess handed the baby over to his own mother. "Please take this baby and nurse him for me, and I will pay you," she said. Smiling happily, Miriam and her mother took their baby home, where he grew up into a fine handsome boy.

One day, they took him back to the princess. She was delighted to see how tall and handsome he had grown, and said that she would like him to come to live in the palace and work for her. "I shall call him Moses," she said.

Carnival
An imprint of the Children's Division
of the Collins Publishing Group
8 Grafton Street, London W1X 3LA

Published by Carnival 1988

Text © 1986 William Collins Sons & Co. Ltd.
Illustrations © 1986 Sally Holmes

ISBN 0 00 194465 7

Printed & bound in Great Britain by
PURNELL BOOK PRODUCTION LIMITED
A MEMBER OF BPCC plc